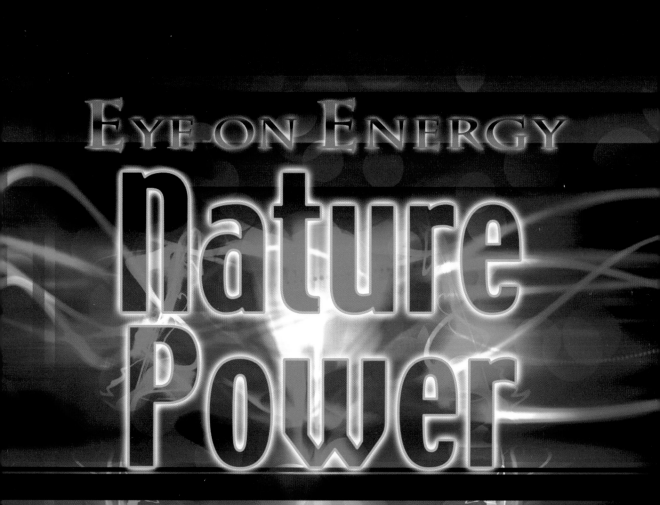

Eye on Energy

Nature Power

ABDO
Publishing Company

Jill C. Wheeler

visit us at
www.abdopublishing.com

Printed in the United States.

Cover Photo: Peter Arnold
Interior Photos: Alamy p. 16; AP Images pp. 4, 8, 11, 21, 24, 27; Corbis pp. 7, 9, 20; Getty Images pp. 18, 19, 23, 25; Ocean Power Delivery p. 15; Peter Arnold pp. 5, 10, 12, 13

Series Coordinator: Rochelle Baltzer
Editors: Rochelle Baltzer, Megan M. Gunderson
Art Direction & Cover Design: Neil Klinepier

Library of Congress Cataloging-in-Publication Data

Wheeler, Jill C., 1964-
  Nature power / Jill C. Wheeler.
    p. cm. – (Eye on energy)
  Includes index.
  ISBN 978–1–59928–806–2
  1. Renewable energy sources–Juvenile literature. I. Title.

  TJ808.2.W44 2007
  621.042–dc22

                                                    2007007111

CONTENTS

Natural Energy

The greatest known sources of energy can be found in the sun and below the earth's surface. These energy providers have been pumping out heat, steam, and light for billions of years.

Our solar system's biggest energy source is the sun. Within the sun, ongoing **nuclear fusion** continuously pumps out 386 billion billion **megawatts** of energy. Just one of those megawatts is enough energy to power 1,000 U.S. homes!

Energy from fusion within the sun takes 1 million years to reach the sun's surface!

The sun's energy supports all life on Earth. It allows plants and animals to live and grow. Fossil fuels, such as coal, oil, and natural gas, were created from ancient plant and animal remains. That means these fuels would not exist without the sun. The sun is also responsible for our planet's weather. That weather affects other energy sources, including winds and tides.

Below its surface, the earth has lots of energy in the form of heat. Scientists estimate that Earth's temperature 50 to 60 miles (80 to 97 km) below the surface is 1,200 to 2,200 degrees Fahrenheit (650 to 1,200°C). Just a small amount of that heat escapes to the surface. The heat we receive from geothermal sources such as **geysers** (GEYE-zuhrz) and hot springs is only 1/20,000 of the heat we get from the sun!

Old Faithful is North America's most famous geyser. Between 3,700 and 8,400 gallons (14,000 and 31,800 L) of hot water shoots out during a single eruption!

SOLAR POWER

For thousands of years, people have used the sun's energy for heat and light. The modern challenge is to **efficiently** turn this solar energy into electricity. Sun-produced heat can warm air or create steam to spin **turbines** to make electricity. Yet, the most promising technology uses solar cells to produce electricity directly from sunlight.

Solar cells, or photovoltaic (foh-toh-vahl-TAY-ihk) cells, directly convert sunlight into energy. Sunlight energizes the **electrons** in solar cells. In response, the energized electrons break free of the bond holding them on the cell.

Solar cells use special materials to encourage the breakaway electrons to move in the same direction. When many electrons do this, an **electric current** is created.

Solar energy does not release **greenhouse gases**. Therefore, it does not add to **global warming**. And, solar energy is **renewable**. For the past ten years, solar cell production has increased about 32 percent every year. Still, less than 1 percent of the world's electricity is produced from solar cells.

The earth receives more energy from the sun in just one hour than the world uses in an entire year! Photovoltaic cell panels harness some of that energy.

In Sydney, Australia, some boats are powered by solar panels in the form of "wings." These wings track the sun and the wind to get the most amount of power from both.

Many solar cells are required to produce a sufficient amount of electricity. And, solar cells are not very **efficient**. Most are able to convert only about 15 percent of their received energy into electricity.

For those reasons, solar cells work better to power devices that do not require much electricity. For example, many hand-held calculators are solar powered.

Solar cell power has another disadvantage. Making solar cell panels is expensive. Therefore, solar-produced electricity costs twice as much as that produced by any other fuel.

Often, solar power is the best option for rural areas without access to other energy sources. However, solar power does not work at night. It is not as effective on cloudy days either. And, some parts of the world do not receive enough sunlight to make solar power a valuable energy source.

In Chad, Africa, refugees learn how to use solar stoves for cooking. Rather than using fuel, solar stoves reflect and capture sunlight to heat food.

SOLAR POWER IN DEVELOPING NATIONS

Throughout the world, about 1.6 billion people do not have access to electricity. Many of them live in developing countries. These places have less advanced economies and more limited access to resources than developed countries, such as the United States or Canada. In developing countries, solar energy is increasingly being used to provide power. This is because solar power is free to operate and available for use in most places.

In some developing countries, people use solar box cookers. These cookers use the sun's heat to cook food. They can also be used to boil drinking water, which leads to fewer diseases and deaths.

Other projects include solar-powered refrigerators, communications systems, and lamps. In some places, solar-powered light-emitting diode (LED) lamps have replaced kerosene oil lamps. LED lamps burn cleaner and longer than kerosene lamps. More than 4,000 LED lamps have been distributed to people in Pakistan, India, Afghanistan, and Guatemala.

IMPROVED CELLS

Today, most solar cells are made from **silicon**. Nothing else works quite as well to make breakaway **electrons** move in the same direction. However, silicon-based solar cells can be expensive. So, researchers are studying cheaper, more **efficient** solar cells. The key is finding an alternative to silicon.

Scientists have now found a way to use plastics for solar cells. A chemical is added to a plastic solar cell. Then, the cell is baked in an oven. This process allows it to more efficiently turn solar energy into

Technicians continue to produce new and improved solar cells.

electricity. Silicon-based solar cells are still more efficient than plastic solar cells. However, plastic solar cells are far less costly.

Another solar cell technology uses nanotubes to make the electrons move easier inside the cell. Nanotubes are tiny **cylinders**. Each one's **diameter** is about 50,000 times smaller than the width of a human hair!

These new technologies may mean more uses for solar power in the future. Already, a Netherlands-based company makes a solar-powered charger for cellular telephones and digital music players such as iPods.

The Soldius1 works with most electronic devices. In direct sunlight, this pocket-sized charger can recharge a device in two to three hours.

WATER POWER

The waterwheel was one of the first mechanical energy sources to replace humans and animals.

Hydropower uses the force of running or falling water as energy. People have been using this force to make energy for thousands of years. More than 2,000 years ago, Greeks used waterwheels to grind wheat into flour.

In 1880, the first hydroelectric power plant was built in England. Today, hydroelectric power is the most used **renewable** energy source to generate electricity. Yet in the United States, it is still not as widely used as nonrenewable energy sources, such as coal or oil. In 2004, hydroelectric power produced 7 percent of the country's electricity.

Hydroelectric power plants most commonly use the energy of restrained water. A dam holds and releases water. Released water spins **turbines**, creating an **electric current**. The amount of water allowed through a dam can be adjusted. For example, more water is released when people need more electricity, such as on hot days.

The Grand Coulee Dam in Washington is North America's single greatest source of water power. Its four power plants produce enough electricity to supply more than 2 million homes!

Hydroelectric power has many benefits. It does not create **greenhouse gases**. And, fewer and smaller **turbines** are needed to produce the same amount of energy as wind turbines. That is because water is **denser** than wind.

However, hydroelectric power also has disadvantages. Dams can harm landscapes and wildlife. Building a dam on a river changes the amount of water available for other uses. Dams are also expensive to construct. And during a severe **drought** (DROWT), there might not be enough water to run the turbines.

OCEAN ENERGY

Most hydroelectric power projects use the force of river water. Yet water in oceans and in bodies of water linked to oceans also has energy. Scientists are developing ways to capture both wave and tidal energy in those places.

A Scotland-based technology called the Pelamis is one type of wave machine. At 490 feet (150 m) long, the Pelamis resembles a giant snake. It stays partly above water and moves with the waves. The Pelamis has **cylinder**-shaped sections linked together by hinged joints. Inside, a motor drives a **generator** to produce electricity.

The world's first "wave farm," or group of wave machines, is taking shape off the coast of northern Portugal. This wave farm uses the Pelamis device. Wave machines are also currently being tested in Hawaii, New Jersey, Scotland, England, and western Australia.

The Pelamis uses energy from waves to make electricity. It operates in waters about 165 to 195 feet (50 to 60 m) deep. And, it is generally placed three to six miles (5 to 10 km) from shore.

Tidal power uses underwater **turbines** that spin like windmills. The force of incoming and outgoing tides turns the turbine blades to produce electricity. Tidal turbines are being installed off the shores of Norway and New York.

Wave and tidal power have several advantages. Ocean waves never stop, so this energy will not run out. And, wave and tidal power do not produce **greenhouse gases**. Therefore, they do not contribute to **global warming**.

However, wave and tidal power can only help places near oceans. Areas with the strongest waves and tides benefit most from this energy. For example, experts believe wave and tidal power might someday produce up to 20 percent of England's electricity.

Like all energy sources, wave and tidal power have downsides. Some machines are very large and must be placed near shorelines. Critics say they look ugly and may discourage tourism. Others worry that underwater turbines might hurt fish and other sea life.

An underwater turbine off England's coast is raised for maintenance. It is part of the Seaflow Project, run by an England-based company.

ROOSEVELT ISLAND TIDAL ENERGY PROJECT

New York City residents may one day obtain electricity from underwater turbines in the city's East River.

ENERGY CAPACITY: The project will produce up to 10 megawatts of power, which is enough electricity to supply the needs of 8,000 homes.

TIMELINE: The project's first underwater turbines began an 18-month test in late 2006.

CONCERNS: Some people fear the underwater turbines may harm fish. However, the project uses slow-turning turbines that are spaced far apart. This helps fish avoid injuries. Also, an underwater sonar system is being used to watch fish activity near the turbines at all times. This helps researchers determine ways to improve the technology to protect fish.

HOW IT WORKS: Large turbines are placed 40 feet (12 m) below the river's surface. The river's strong current turns the turbine blades. The blades spin up to 32 times per minute, depending on the flow of water. This motion drives a generator to produce electricity.

HIGHLIGHTS: The Roosevelt Island project is the first tidal energy test in the United States. The first electricity produced from the project will power a nearby supermarket and parking garage.

The East River is actually a strait. It connects two parts of the nearby Atlantic Ocean.

CAPTURING WIND

Just as the sun creates weather to make waves and tides, it also causes wind. People have been using wind to produce energy for thousands of years. Egyptians used wind-powered sailing ships as early as 2800 BC.

Windmills most likely originated in Persia, now Iran, in the AD 600s. These machines use the power of wind to operate. Most windmills were first used for simple tasks such as grinding grain, pumping water, and sawing wood. Some windmills are still used today.

A pinwheel captures wind in the same way that a windmill does.

Windmills used to make electricity are called wind **turbines**. Wind turbines have long blades at the top of tall towers. Winds

FACT OR FICTION?

The United States ranks third in the world in wind power capacity.

Fact. Only Germany and Spain have higher wind power capacities.

are stronger farther from the ground, so towers must be tall. Wind spins the blades. This motion drives a **generator**, which creates an **electric current**.

Some countries use wind power more than others. In Denmark, it provides 20 percent of the country's electricity needs. However, wind power accounts for less than 1 percent of energy both in the United States and worldwide.

Wind turbines that are placed in large clusters are part of a wind farm. Wind farms are also called wind power plants.

Unlike other power plants, many wind farms are owned and operated by businesspeople. Owners sell the electricity produced at their wind farms to electric utilities.

Wind farms are constructed where winds are steady and strong. A site must have a minimum yearly average wind speed of between 11 and 13 miles per hour (18 and 21 km/h).

Areas near mountain passes are ideal locations for wind farms. The tops of rounded hills, open plains, or shorelines are also good spots for wind farms.

California is one of the highest wind power producers in the United States. This wind farm in the San Bernardino Mountains contains more than 4,000 wind turbines!

In the United States, wind power has become increasingly popular. There are now wind **turbines** in 30 states. In August 2006, the country's wind-generating **capacity** reached 10,000 **megawatts**. That is enough energy to power more than 2.5 million homes!

Many locations in New England have good wind resources. Mount Washington, in New Hampshire, has the highest recorded wind speed in the mainland United States.

There are numerous benefits to using wind power. Wind-produced electricity does not create pollution or **greenhouse gases**. Wind is free. And, there is no danger that it will run out.

However, wind power is not always reliable. Some areas may not receive strong enough winds to produce electricity. And, even areas with strong winds may not be windy all of the time.

There are other drawbacks, too. Spinning turbine blades are dangerous for birds. And, some people think landscapes dotted with tall towers and spinning blades are noisy and unattractive.

Researchers are working to address some of these concerns. New wind turbine and tower designs make the most of lower wind speeds. Slower spinning makes turbines safer for birds.

As for the eyesore complaint, research has found that the more people favor **renewable** energy, the better wind **turbines** look to them. So the more people know about wind power's benefits, the less they will mind seeing the towers!

An average wind turbine has three blades, each 200 feet (61 m) long.

21

WIND ON WATER

Some of Earth's windier places are not on dry land. They are off coasts, over water. Wind is stronger and more regular in many of those areas. That means energy production for wind farms is higher off shores than on land. And like onshore wind farms, offshore farms generate electricity without creating **greenhouse gases**.

These windy locations may seem like ideal places to set up wind **turbines**. The largest offshore facility is in Denmark. This wind farm has 72 turbines. The turbines rise 360 feet (110 m) above the North Sea. They produce enough electricity to power 145,000 homes.

Several U.S. companies are developing offshore wind farm projects off the New England coast. However, many people oppose these farms. Critics say wind farms would spoil the look of the coast. They worry that the farms would damage the local **economy**. They fear that tourists would not want to visit a beach where wind turbines could be seen in the distance.

Other people fear constructing a wind farm would disturb the sensitive ocean **environment**. Likewise, the sea environment can easily damage equipment. So, offshore **turbines** require more maintenance and need faster replacement than onshore turbines. The location of a wind farm might also be a problem for boats and ships.

Some people fear that wind turbines near shorelines might stop people from vacationing in those areas. If that happened, local businesses would lose the money they depend on from tourists.

HEAT IN THE EARTH

Geothermal energy comes from heat below the earth's surface. Most of that heat never escapes from underground. Yet, some is released through volcanoes, hot springs, **geysers**, and vents.

People have been using geothermal energy for thousands of years. Some Roman homes were heated by natural hot springs more than 2,000 years ago. Early civilizations also used geothermal energy to cook, fire clay pots, and make baths and spas.

The first geothermal power plant was built in 1904 in Landrello, Italy. Today, 24 countries obtain energy from geothermal sources. In Iceland, 85 percent of homes are heated with geothermal energy!

Romans founded Bath, England, on the site of hot springs. Today, tourists can see where the Romans once gathered to enjoy the hot springs

Geothermal power plants obtain energy from wells that reach deep into the earth. Some wells bring up either steam or hot water to turn into steam. The steam drives **turbines**, which produce an **electric current**. Other wells pump water down onto hot rocks to create steam to drive turbines.

Bathers can enjoy Iceland's Blue Lagoon geothermal seawater. Nearby, a geothermal power plant produces electricity. In Iceland, 45 percent of all energy comes from geothermal sources.

In the past, geothermal energy usage was limited by geography. Many parts of the world do not have usable geothermal resources. Yet, new technologies are making geothermal energy available in more places.

One technology may allow some "cooler" geothermal spots to produce energy. It combines water from such areas and a special liquid called R134a. R134a boils at a low temperature. So when the two are combined, the cooler water is hot enough to turn R134a liquid into gas. Just like steam, the gas is used to drive a **turbine**.

This method might also create a way to produce geothermal energy from other deep wells. For example, some oil wells bring up warm water as well as oil. By using R143a liquid, the warm water could possibly help produce geothermal energy.

There are several advantages to geothermal energy. It does not create **greenhouse gases** that contribute to **global warming**. And although geothermal power plants are expensive to build, they are inexpensive to operate.

Geothermal energy is generally considered a **renewable** energy source. However, some geothermal spots have seen a decrease in water volume or pressure throughout the years. But, cool water can be pumped back into a geothermal system to maintain water levels.

The United States produces 32 percent of the world's geothermal electricity. That's more than any other country! The Geysers Geothermal Field in northern California generates enough power to supply a city the size of San Francisco.

HEAT PUMPS

People who do not live near geothermally active places can still use geothermal energy to heat and cool their homes. That is because the upper ten feet (3 m) of most of the earth's surface stays between 50 and 60 degrees Fahrenheit (10 and 16°C).

A geothermal heat pump uses this constant temperature to heat and cool buildings. The system pumps water through underground piping. Underground, the water is regulated to Earth's temperature, which is warmer than winter air and cooler than summer air.

The water is then pumped over coils containing refrigerant, which absorbs the water's heat. Next, the refrigerant is heated using pressure. This heat is sent into the building. In summer, hot air from the building is sent back out through the same system.

Heat pumps can be installed in new or existing homes. Pipes can be buried in large grids across a backyard. Or, they can be run down deep wells. People who live near a pond can put a series of pipes there, too. That is often the least costly option.

Heat pumps are more expensive to install than ordinary heating and cooling systems. It generally takes three to ten years for fuel savings to equal the cost of pipes and installation. But after that, heat pumps save about $300 to $800 per year in energy costs for most homes.

Systems such as heat pumps take advantage of natural, **renewable** energy. This type of energy is not as harmful to the **environment** as fossil fuel energy. Experts continue to research technologies and designs that use natural energy. With increasing interest in nature power, more new and improved systems are becoming a reality.

5 ROOM AIR GOES BACK INTO SYSTEM

COLD OUTSIDE AIR

4 WARMED AIR TRAVELS INTO ROOMS

GEOTHERMAL EXCHANGE SYSTEM IN HEATING MODE

WARM GROUND

3 HEAT CIRCULATES INTO HOUSE

1 UNDERGROUND PIPES ABSORB HEAT FROM EARTH

2 REFRIGERANT ABSORBS HEAT

GLOSSARY

capacity - the power to perform or to produce.

cylinder - a solid figure of two parallel circles bound by a curved surface. A soda can is an example of a cylinder.

dense - having a high mass per unit volume.

diameter - the distance across the middle of an object, such as a circle.

drought - a long period of dry weather.

economy - the way a nation uses its money, goods, and natural resources.

efficient - the ability to produce a desired result, especially without wasting time or energy.

electric current - a flow of electric charge.

electron - one of the main parts of an atom. It is negatively charged and travels around the nucleus, or center, of an atom.

environment - all the surroundings that affect the growth and well-being of a living thing.

generator - a machine that changes mechanical energy into electrical energy.

geyser - a spring that sends up occasional fountainlike jets of hot water and steam into the air.

global warming - an increase in the average temperature of Earth's surface.

greenhouse gas - a gas, such as carbon dioxide, that traps heat in the atmosphere.

megawatt - one million watts. A watt is a unit of electric power that equals the work done at the rate of one joule per second.

nuclear fusion - the joining of the nuclei of two lightweight chemical elements to form the nucleus of a heavier one.

renewable - able to replenish naturally in a relatively short period of time. Renewable energy resources include biomass, hydropower, geothermal energy, wind energy, and solar energy.

silicon - a chemical element found in sand, clay, soil, and almost all rocks. It is used in many computers and other electronics.

turbine - a device with rotating blades that are turned by a moving force, such as water, steam, gas, or wind. It turns the energy of movement into mechanical power.

WEB SITES

To learn more about nature power, visit ABDO Publishing Company on the World Wide Web at **www.abdopublishing.com**. Web sites about nature power are featured on our Book Links page. These links are routinely monitored and updated to provide the most current information available.

INDEX